RECOGNIZING GOD'S DIRECTIONS IN YOUR LIFE

JEREMIAH 29:11

A JOURNAL

Recognizing God's Directions in Your Life: Jeremiah 29:11
A Journal

For information about this title or to order other books and/or electronic media, contact the publisher:

AJ Sam
theajsam.com
theajsam@gmail.com

ISBN: 979-8-9869467-4-0

Printed in the United States of America
Cover and Interior design: 1106 Design

Introduction

"For I know the plans I have for you," says the Lord. "They are plans for good and not for disaster, to give you a future and a hope." (Jeremiah 29:11 NLT)

As I consider the goodness of God, I am overwhelmed with its height, depth, and breadth. I think about the times He brought me out of harm's way. I think about the times He has provided for all of my needs and many of my wants.

I think about the times He made my enemies my footstool! And I think about the times He made a way out of no way.

There have been times God led me on journeys I would have ***never*** taken on my own, but in the end, realized they were just the journeys I ***needed*** to take. These journeys collectively made me a better husband, a better father, a better son, a better sibling, a better friend, a better teacher, a better preacher, and most of all—a better human being.

This portion of scripture speaks to the idea of God's purpose for your life, His plan for your life, one that brings hope, prosperity, and a meaningful future. You will have moments of uncertainty and struggles, but this scripture reminds you that there is a higher purpose for your life. When you face obstacles, feel lost, or when the path is unclear, it inspires you to keep faith that the challenges are part of a greater plan, not for disaster but for growth.

Perhaps you're searching for direction in areas like relationships, finances, health, love, purpose, and personal development. With God's guidance, there is a positive outcome for each aspect, so trusting the journey, no matter how difficult, is crucial.

Just as a compass guides a traveler, this scripture reinforces the idea that God's love and care are guiding you, steering you toward a hopeful future.

The compass on the cover reflects the idea of navigating life while trusting that you are moving in the direction of a meaningful plan—God's plan for your future. Just like traversing a vast ocean, or a dense forest, or a desolate desert with nothing more than a compass and God, you can trust that the direction you are taking is true.

"For I know the plans I have for you," says the Lord. "They are plans for good and not for disaster, to give you a future and a hope." (Jeremiah 29:11 NLT)

Several years ago my daughter, Ya'Shantaye, in the midst of a very difficult time for me, gave me a journal as a gift. I wrote in that journal daily for a year.

My wife and I recently relocated to the Tampa Bay area of Florida, and in getting rid of items that I'd carried around with me for years, I rediscovered the journal. Although more than five years had passed, the words were as fresh and healing as the days I wrote those notes to myself. And it reminded me of the power of Jeremiah 29:11.

"I know the plans I have for you . . ."

God knows, He understands, He designs, He purposes these plans for me as an individual. These are plans for me and no one else. And the awesomeness is that He has specific plans for you as well.

"They are plans for good and not for disaster . . ."

In spite of what it may appear to be at that time, no matter how difficult it is at that time, no matter how hurtful it is at that time, it is always for good—sometimes for our good, other times for the good of others. But most importantly, the plan God fashions for each of us ***won't*** end in disaster.

"To give you a future and a hope."

God wants the best for us. God wants the best from us. God wants the best out of us. God's demands are appropriate because He put the best in us.

Many times, though, getting the best requires us to take journeys through the valley of the shadow of death, through a fiery furnace, through a lion's den, through the belly of a sea creature, or through the muck and the mire.

Other times it means we must take journeys through physical pain, through emotional heartache, through public embarrassment, through this journey we call—life. But with God, we always have a future, and we always have hope.

"For I know the plans I have for you," says the Lord. "They are plans for good and not for disaster, to give you a future and a hope." (Jeremiah 29:11 NLT)

Along with Jeremiah 29:11, I'm reminded of the following scriptures . . .

"Trust in the Lord with all your heart. And do not lean on your own understanding. In all your ways acknowledge Him, And He will make your paths straight." (Proverbs 3:5–6)

"And we know that all things work together for good to them that love God, to them who are the called according to His purpose." (Romans 8:28)

Add to these scriptures the fact that God is omnipresent, we can begin to grasp the truth that all the points on the compass lead us to God. No matter if we're going there with tears of joy or sorrow. No matter if we're going there freely or reluctantly. No matter if we're going there intentionally or by chance.

No matter if we're striding there or being dragged. No matter if we're going there bruised, beaten, and battered. No matter if we're going there victorious, triumphant, or successful. God is always the destination of our journey.

It is when we recognize God's direction in our lives that we discover hope for our future. This verse offers encouragement that every step, especially the difficult ones, lead you toward a good and purposeful future—one filled with hope.

It is my prayer that you find this journal helpful in traversing the journey God has created just for you. It is my prayer that you find insight not only from scripture, but from daily situations, from friends, from families, and even from foes. And it is my prayer that you find insight from within yourself.

It is my prayer that you end your days as I have begun to end mine. Reflecting on the goodness of God, the promises of God, the mercy of God, and the grace of God. That with understanding God's purpose for your life and the reason for your journey, you are better equipped to recognize, to "see God working," in all circumstances along the way. It is my prayer that God blesses you and yours with an abundant life. With a vibrant ministry, and with a testimony that changes the world. Enjoy ***your*** journey.

Yours in Christ,
AJ Sam

Meet the Author

Place a picture
of you in this
frame.

Date: ________________

Consider the photo you chose . . .
Why did you choose this photo?
What does this person hope to get out of this journal?

This is the author of this book,
because truly, only you can chronicle your journey.

"For I know the thoughts that I think toward you," saith the Lord, "thoughts of peace, and not of evil, to give you an expected end." (Jer. 29:11 KJV)

"For I know the plans I have for you," declares the Lord, "plans to prosper you and not to harm you, plans to give you hope and a future." (Jer. 29:11 NIV)

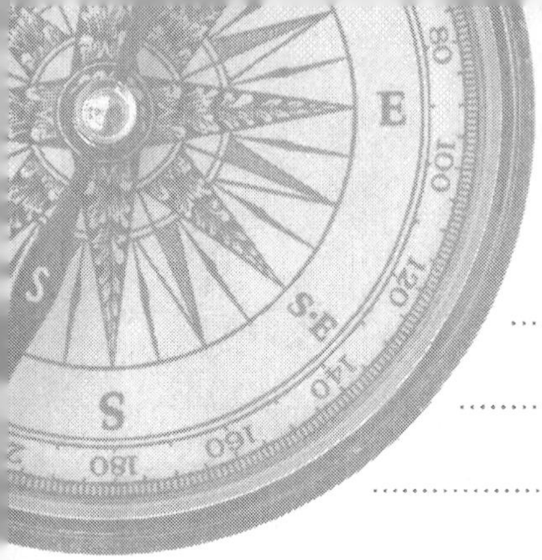

"For I know the plans I have for you," says the Lord. "They are plans for good and not for disaster, to give you a future and a hope." (Jer. 29:11 NLT)

"For I know the thoughts that I think toward you," saith the Lord, "thoughts of peace, and not of evil, to give you an expected end." (Jer. 29:11 KJV)

"For I know the plans I have for you," declares the Lord, "plans to prosper you and not to harm you, plans to give you hope and a future." (Jer. 29:11 NIV)

"For I know the plans I have for you," says the Lord. "They are plans for good and not for disaster, to give you a future and a hope." (Jer. 29:11 NLT)

"For I know the thoughts that I think toward you," saith the Lord, "thoughts of peace, and not of evil, to give you an expected end." (Jer. 29:11 KJV)

"For I know the plans I have for you," declares the Lord, "plans to prosper you and not to harm you, plans to give you hope and a future." (Jer. 29:11 NIV)

"For I know the plans I have for you," says the Lord. "They are plans for good and not for disaster, to give you a future and a hope." (Jer. 29:11 NLT)

"For I know the thoughts that I think toward you," saith the Lord, "thoughts of peace, and not of evil, to give you an expected end." (Jer. 29:11 KJV)

"For I know the plans I have for you," declares the Lord, "plans to prosper you and not to harm you, plans to give you hope and a future." (Jer. 29:11 NIV)

"For I know the plans I have for you," says the Lord. "They are plans for good and not for disaster, to give you a future and a hope." (Jer. 29:11 NLT)

"For I know the thoughts that I think toward you," saith the Lord, "thoughts of peace, and not of evil, to give you an expected end." (Jer. 29:11 KJV)

"For I know the plans I have for you," declares the Lord, "plans to prosper you and not to harm you, plans to give you hope and a future." (Jer. 29:11 NIV)

"For I know the plans I have for you," says the Lord. "They are plans for good and not for disaster, to give you a future and a hope." (Jer. 29:11 NLT)

"For I know the thoughts that I think toward you," saith the Lord, "thoughts of peace, and not of evil, to give you an expected end." (Jer. 29:11 KJV)

"For I know the plans I have for you," declares the Lord, "plans to prosper you and not to harm you, plans to give you hope and a future." (Jer. 29:11 NIV)

"For I know the plans I have for you," says the Lord. "They are plans for good and not for disaster, to give you a future and a hope." (Jer. 29:11 NLT)

"For I know the thoughts that I think toward you," saith the Lord, "thoughts of peace, and not of evil, to give you an expected end." (Jer. 29:11 KJV)

"For I know the plans I have for you," declares the Lord, "plans to prosper you and not to harm you, plans to give you hope and a future." (Jer. 29:11 NIV)

"For I know the plans I have for you," says the Lord. "They are plans for good and not for disaster, to give you a future and a hope." (Jer. 29:11 NLT)

"For I know the thoughts that I think toward you," saith the Lord, "thoughts of peace, and not of evil, to give you an expected end." (Jer. 29:11 KJV)

"For I know the plans I have for you," declares the Lord, "plans to prosper you and not to harm you, plans to give you hope and a future." (Jer. 29:11 NIV)

"For I know the plans I have for you," says the Lord.
"They are plans for good and not for disaster, to give you
a future and a hope." (Jer. 29:11 NLT)

"For I know the thoughts that I think toward you," saith the Lord, "thoughts of peace, and not of evil, to give you an expected end." (Jer. 29:11 KJV)

"For I know the plans I have for you," declares the Lord, "plans to prosper you and not to harm you, plans to give you hope and a future." (Jer. 29:11 NIV)

"For I know the plans I have for you," says the Lord. "They are plans for good and not for disaster, to give you a future and a hope." (Jer. 29:11 NLT)

"For I know the thoughts that I think toward you," saith the Lord, *"thoughts of peace, and not of evil, to give you an expected end."* *(Jer. 29:11 KJV)*

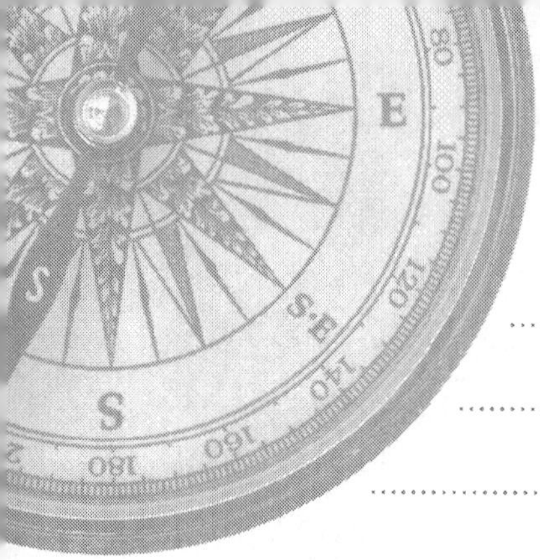

"For I know the plans I have for you," declares the Lord, "plans to prosper you and not to harm you, plans to give you hope and a future." (Jer. 29:11 NIV)

"For I know the plans I have for you," says the Lord. "They are plans for good and not for disaster, to give you a future and a hope." (Jer. 29:11 NLT)

"For I know the thoughts that I think toward you," saith the Lord, "thoughts of peace, and not of evil, to give you an expected end." (Jer. 29:11 KJV)

"For I know the plans I have for you," declares the Lord, "plans to prosper you and not to harm you, plans to give you hope and a future." (Jer. 29:11 NIV)

"For I know the plans I have for you," says the Lord. "They are plans for good and not for disaster, to give you a future and a hope." (Jer. 29:11 NLT)

"For I know the thoughts that I think toward you," saith the Lord, "thoughts of peace, and not of evil, to give you an expected end."
(Jer. 29:11 KJV)

"For I know the plans I have for you," declares the Lord, "plans to prosper you and not to harm you, plans to give you hope and a future." (Jer. 29:11 NIV)

"For I know the plans I have for you," says the Lord. "They are plans for good and not for disaster, to give you a future and a hope." (Jer. 29:11 NLT)

"For I know the thoughts that I think toward you," saith the Lord, "thoughts of peace, and not of evil, to give you an expected end." (Jer. 29:11 KJV)

"For I know the plans I have for you," declares the Lord, "plans to prosper you and not to harm you, plans to give you hope and a future." (Jer. 29:11 NIV)

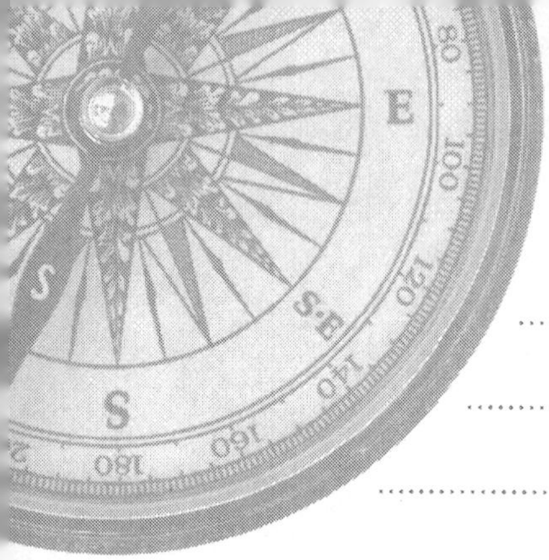

"For I know the plans I have for you," says the Lord. "They are plans for good and not for disaster, to give you a future and a hope." (Jer. 29:11 NLT)

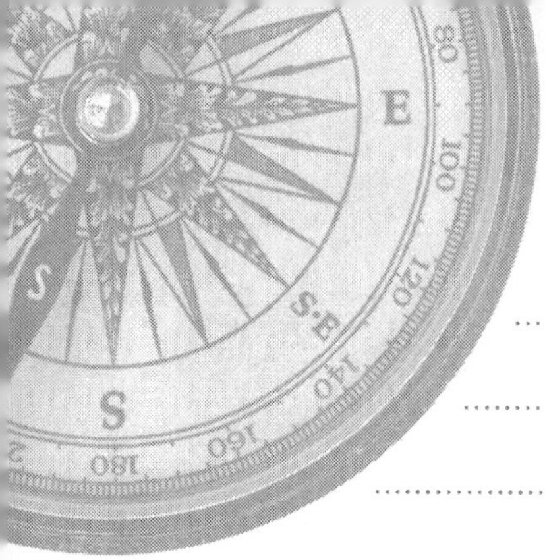

"For I know the thoughts that I think toward you," saith the Lord, "thoughts of peace, and not of evil, to give you an expected end." (Jer. 29:11 KJV)

"For I know the plans I have for you," declares the Lord, "plans to prosper you and not to harm you, plans to give you hope and a future." (Jer. 29:11 NIV)

"For I know the plans I have for you," says the Lord. "They are plans for good and not for disaster, to give you a future and a hope." (Jer. 29:11 NLT)

"For I know the thoughts that I think toward you," saith the Lord, "thoughts of peace, and not of evil, to give you an expected end." (Jer. 29:11 KJV)

"For I know the plans I have for you," declares the Lord, "plans to prosper you and not to harm you, plans to give you hope and a future." (Jer. 29:11 NIV)

"For I know the plans I have for you," says the Lord. "They are plans for good and not for disaster, to give you a future and a hope." (Jer. 29:11 NLT)

"For I know the thoughts that I think toward you," saith the Lord, "thoughts of peace, and not of evil, to give you an expected end." (Jer. 29:11 KJV)

"For I know the plans I have for you," declares the Lord, "plans to prosper you and not to harm you, plans to give you hope and a future." (Jer. 29:11 NIV)

"For I know the plans I have for you," says the Lord. "They are plans for good and not for disaster, to give you a future and a hope." (Jer. 29:11 NLT)

"For I know the thoughts that I think toward you," saith the Lord, "thoughts of peace, and not of evil, to give you an expected end." (Jer. 29:11 KJV)

"For I know the plans I have for you," declares the Lord, "plans to prosper you and not to harm you, plans to give you hope and a future." (Jer. 29:11 NIV)

"For I know the plans I have for you," says the Lord. "They are plans for good and not for disaster, to give you a future and a hope." (Jer. 29:11 NLT)

"For I know the thoughts that I think toward you," saith the Lord, "thoughts of peace, and not of evil, to give you an expected end." (Jer. 29:11 KJV)

"For I know the plans I have for you," declares the Lord, "plans to prosper you and not to harm you, plans to give you hope and a future." (Jer. 29:11 NIV)

"For I know the plans I have for you," says the Lord. "They are plans for good and not for disaster, to give you a future and a hope." (Jer. 29:11 NLT)

"For I know the thoughts that I think toward you," saith the Lord, "thoughts of peace, and not of evil, to give you an expected end." (Jer. 29:11 KJV)

"For I know the plans I have for you," declares the Lord, "plans to prosper you and not to harm you, plans to give you hope and a future." (Jer. 29:11 NIV)

"For I know the plans I have for you," says the Lord. "They are plans for good and not for disaster, to give you a future and a hope." (Jer. 29:11 NLT)

"For I know the thoughts that I think toward you," saith the Lord, "thoughts of peace, and not of evil, to give you an expected end."
(Jer. 29:11 KJV)

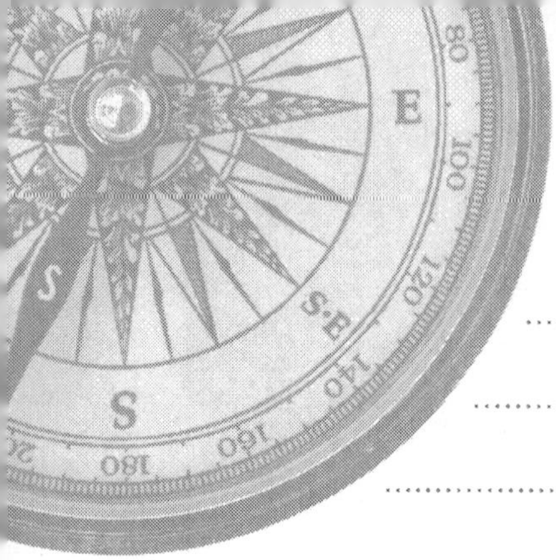

"For I know the plans I have for you," declares the Lord, "plans to prosper you and not to harm you, plans to give you hope and a future." (Jer. 29:11 NIV)

"For I know the plans I have for you," says the Lord. "They are plans for good and not for disaster, to give you a future and a hope." (Jer. 29:11 NLT)

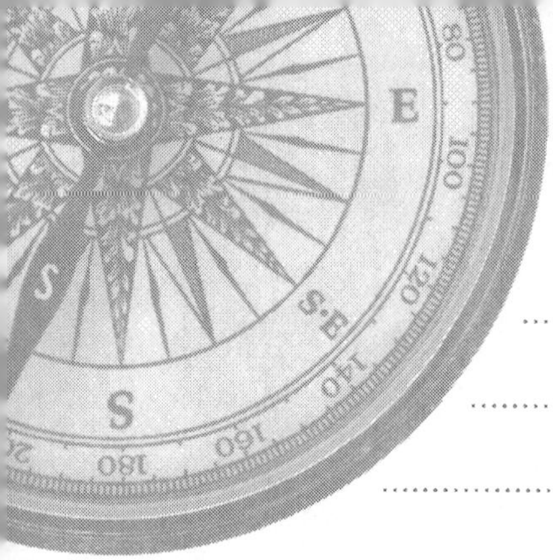

"For I know the thoughts that I think toward you," saith the Lord, "thoughts of peace, and not of evil, to give you an expected end." (Jer. 29:11 KJV)

"For I know the plans I have for you," declares the Lord, "plans to prosper you and not to harm you, plans to give you hope and a future." (Jer. 29:11 NIV)

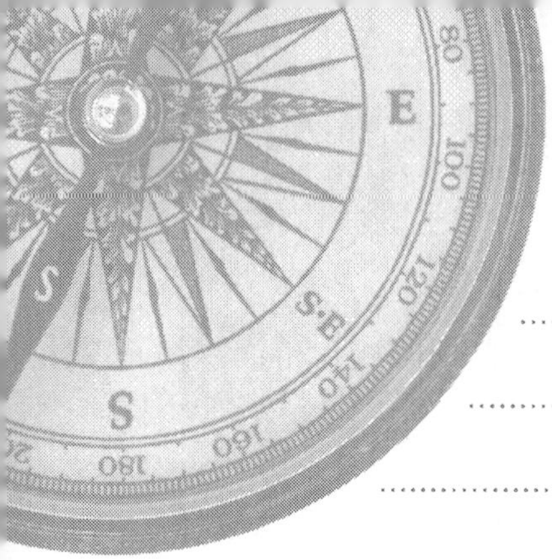

"For I know the plans I have for you," says the Lord. "They are plans for good and not for disaster, to give you a future and a hope." (Jer. 29:11 NLT)

"For I know the thoughts that I think toward you," saith the Lord, "thoughts of peace, and not of evil, to give you an expected end." *(Jer. 29:11 KJV)*

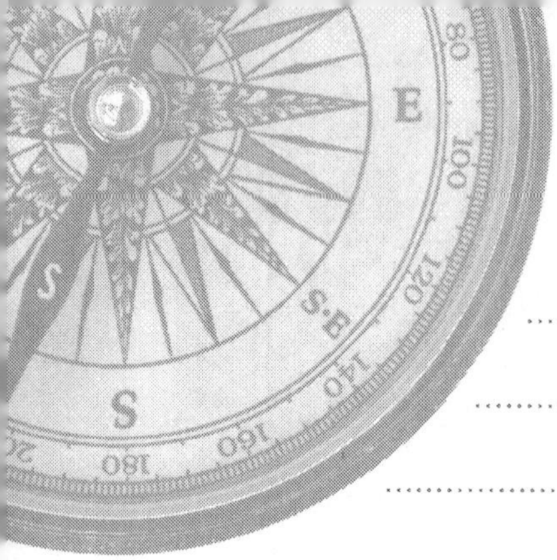

"For I know the plans I have for you," declares the Lord, "plans to prosper you and not to harm you, plans to give you hope and a future." (Jer. 29:11 NIV)

"For I know the plans I have for you," says the Lord. "They are plans for good and not for disaster, to give you a future and a hope." (Jer. 29:11 NLT)

"For I know the thoughts that I think toward you," saith the Lord, "thoughts of peace, and not of evil, to give you an expected end." (Jer. 29:11 KJV)

"For I know the plans I have for you," declares the Lord, "plans to prosper you and not to harm you, plans to give you hope and a future." (Jer. 29:11 NIV)

"For I know the plans I have for you," says the Lord. "They are plans for good and not for disaster, to give you a future and a hope." (Jer. 29:11 NLT)

"For I know the thoughts that I think toward you," saith the Lord,
"thoughts of peace, and not of evil, to give you an expected end."
(Jer. 29:11 KJV)

"For I know the plans I have for you," declares the Lord, "plans to prosper you and not to harm you, plans to give you hope and a future." (Jer. 29:11 NIV)

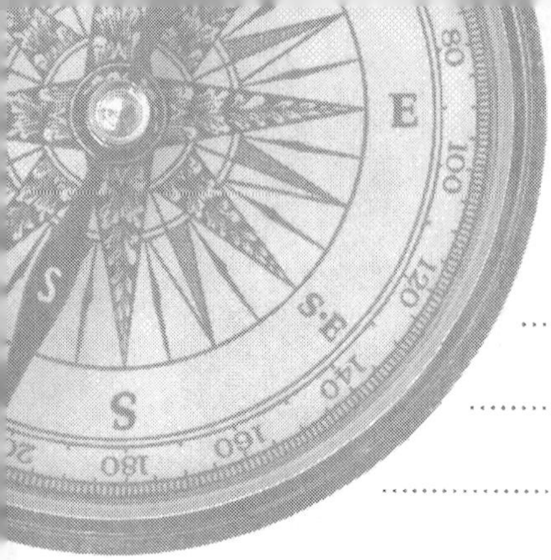

"For I know the plans I have for you," says the Lord. "They are plans for good and not for disaster, to give you a future and a hope." (Jer. 29:11 NLT)

"For I know the thoughts that I think toward you," saith the Lord, "thoughts of peace, and not of evil, to give you an expected end." (Jer. 29:11 KJV)

"For I know the plans I have for you," declares the Lord, "plans to prosper you and not to harm you, plans to give you hope and a future." (Jer. 29:11 NIV)

"For I know the plans I have for you," says the Lord. "They are plans for good and not for disaster, to give you a future and a hope." (Jer. 29:11 NLT)

"For I know the thoughts that I think toward you," saith the Lord, "thoughts of peace, and not of evil, to give you an expected end." (Jer. 29:11 KJV)

"For I know the plans I have for you," declares the Lord, "plans to prosper you and not to harm you, plans to give you hope and a future." (Jer. 29:11 NIV)

"For I know the plans I have for you," says the Lord. "They are plans for good and not for disaster, to give you a future and a hope." (Jer. 29:11 NLT)

"For I know the thoughts that I think toward you," saith the Lord, "thoughts of peace, and not of evil, to give you an expected end." (Jer. 29:11 KJV)

"For I know the plans I have for you," declares the Lord, "plans to prosper you and not to harm you, plans to give you hope and a future." (Jer. 29:11 NIV)

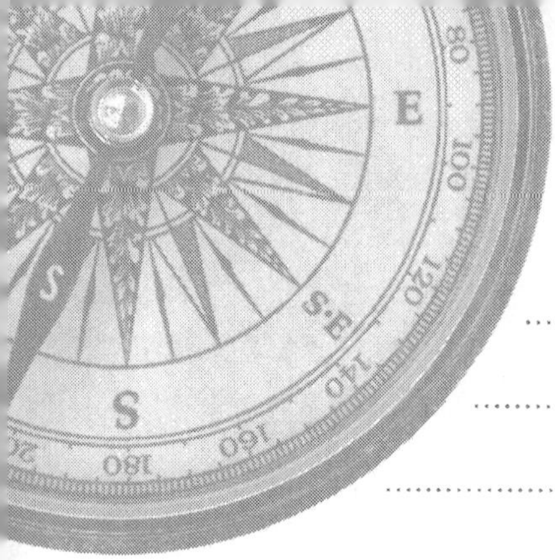

"For I know the plans I have for you," says the Lord. "They are plans for good and not for disaster, to give you a future and a hope." (Jer. 29:11 NLT)

"For I know the thoughts that I think toward you," saith the Lord, "thoughts of peace, and not of evil, to give you an expected end." (Jer. 29:11 KJV)

"For I know the plans I have for you," declares the Lord, "plans to prosper you and not to harm you, plans to give you hope and a future." (Jer. 29:11 NIV)

"For I know the plans I have for you," says the Lord. "They are plans for good and not for disaster, to give you a future and a hope." (Jer. 29:11 NLT)

"For I know the thoughts that I think toward you," saith the Lord, "thoughts of peace, and not of evil, to give you an expected end." (Jer. 29:11 KJV)

"For I know the plans I have for you," declares the Lord, "plans to prosper you and not to harm you, plans to give you hope and a future." (Jer. 29:11 NIV)

"For I know the plans I have for you," says the Lord. "They are plans for good and not for disaster, to give you a future and a hope." (Jer. 29:11 NLT)

"For I know the thoughts that I think toward you," saith the Lord, "thoughts of peace, and not of evil, to give you an expected end." *(Jer. 29:11 KJV)*

"For I know the plans I have for you," declares the Lord, "plans to prosper you and not to harm you, plans to give you hope and a future." (Jer. 29:11 NIV)

"For I know the plans I have for you," says the Lord. "They are plans for good and not for disaster, to give you a future and a hope." (Jer. 29:11 NLT)

"For I know the thoughts that I think toward you," saith the Lord, "thoughts of peace, and not of evil, to give you an expected end." (Jer. 29:11 KJV)

"For I know the plans I have for you," declares the Lord, "plans to prosper you and not to harm you, plans to give you hope and a future." (Jer. 29:11 NIV)

"For I know the plans I have for you," says the Lord. "They are plans for good and not for disaster, to give you a future and a hope." (Jer. 29:11 NLT)

"For I know the thoughts that I think toward you," saith the Lord, "thoughts of peace, and not of evil, to give you an expected end." *(Jer. 29:11 KJV)*

"For I know the plans I have for you," declares the Lord, "plans to prosper you and not to harm you, plans to give you hope and a future." (Jer. 29:11 NIV)

"For I know the plans I have for you," says the Lord. "They are plans for good and not for disaster, to give you a future and a hope." (Jer. 29:11 NLT)

"For I know the thoughts that I think toward you," saith the Lord, "thoughts of peace, and not of evil, to give you an expected end." (Jer. 29:11 KJV)

"For I know the plans I have for you," declares the Lord, "plans to prosper you and not to harm you, plans to give you hope and a future." (Jer. 29:11 NIV)

"For I know the plans I have for you," says the Lord. "They are plans for good and not for disaster, to give you a future and a hope." (Jer. 29:11 NLT)

"For I know the thoughts that I think toward you," saith the Lord, "thoughts of peace, and not of evil, to give you an expected end."
(Jer. 29:11 KJV)

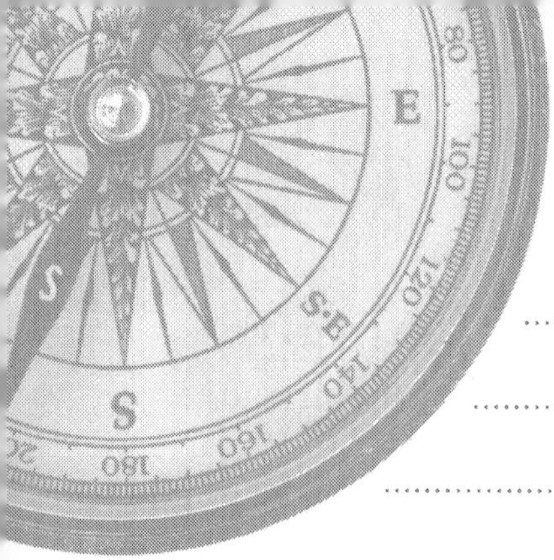

"For I know the plans I have for you," declares the Lord, "plans to prosper you and not to harm you, plans to give you hope and a future." (Jer. 29:11 NIV)

"For I know the plans I have for you," says the Lord. "They are plans for good and not for disaster, to give you a future and a hope." (Jer. 29:11 NLT)

Made in the USA
Columbia, SC
06 February 2025